Workbook

Pockets 2

Second Edition

Mario Herrera   Barbara Hojel

PEARSON
Longman

Pockets 2, Second Edition
Workbook

Pearson Education, 10 Bank Street, White Plains, NY 10606

Staff credits: The people who made up the *Pockets, Second
Edition* team, representing editorial, production, design, and
manufacturing, are Rhea Banker, Iris Candelaria, Tracey Munz
Cataldo, Christine Edmonds, Johnnie Farmer, Nancy Flaggman,
Yoko Mia Hirano, Christopher Leonowicz, Judy Li, Linda Moser,
Barbara Sabella, Susan Saslow, and Mairead Stack.
Text design: Tracey Munz Cataldo
Text composition: TSI Graphics
Text font: Frutiger Bold
Illustrations: Javier Montiel

PEARSON LONGMAN ON THE **WEB**

Pearsonlongman.com offers online
resources for teachers and students. Access
our Companion Websites, our online catalog,
and our local offices around the world.

Visit us at **pearsonlongman.com**.

ISBN-10: 0-13-603853-0
ISBN-13: 978-0-13-603853-5

Printed in China
24 18

Contents

1 At School 2

2 Our Senses 10

3 At the Fair 18

4 People We Know 26

5 Zoo Animals 34

6 Clothes for All Weather 42

7 Foods We Like 50

8 Our Neighborhood 58

9 The Sky 66

Extra Practice: Reading and Writing 75

Smiley Tiger Puppet 93

1 At School

Inside or *outside*? Say and match.

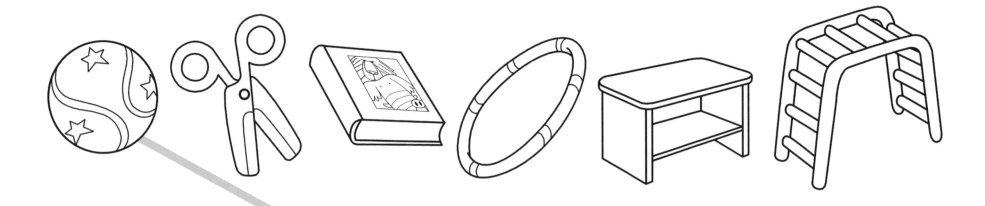

Draw someone climbing the jungle gym.

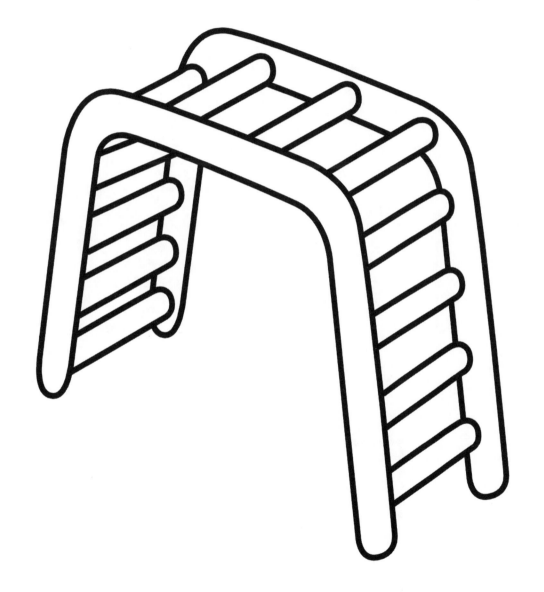

Trace. Make objects with the shapes.

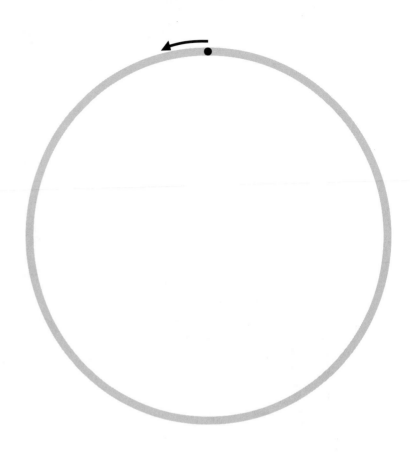

Practice

What is he/she doing? Say. Color *outside* activities green and *inside* activities yellow.

Trace. Match and color.

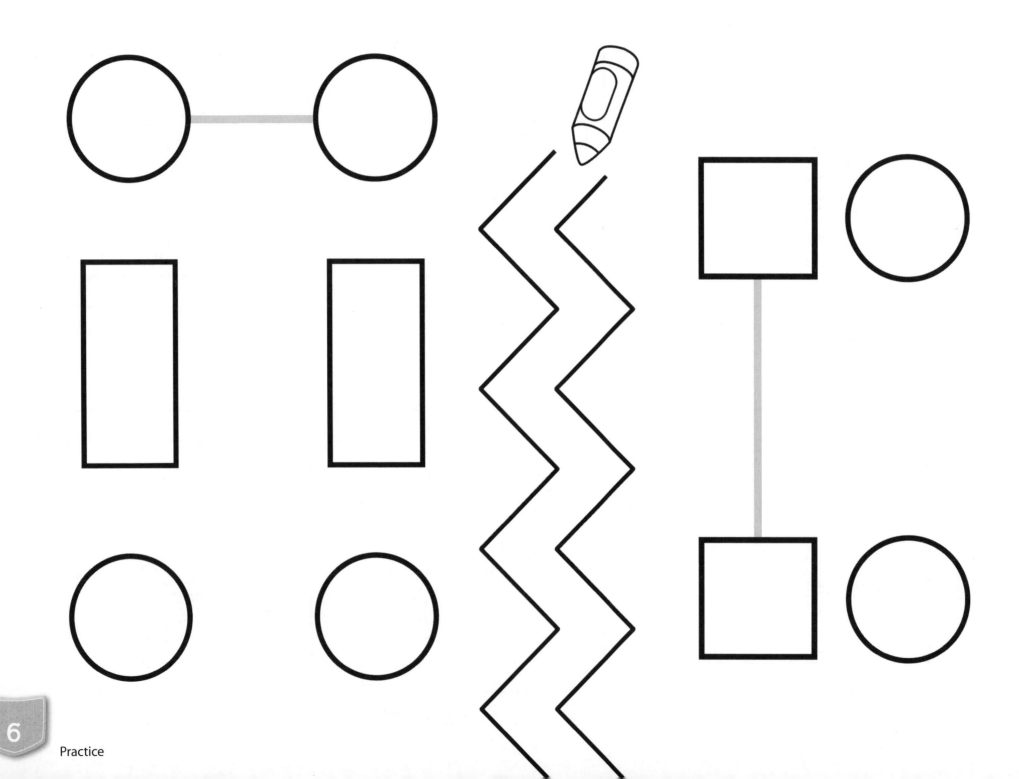

Practice

In or *out*? Point and say. Draw something *in* the hoop.

Our Values

Draw your face or paste in your photo.

Application/Value: Work Together

At School

Draw a playground and a classroom.

Our Senses

2

Name the senses and match.

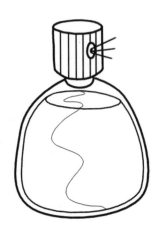

Warm Up

Trace. Circle items you can hear. Say.

Trace. Cross out items you can't taste. Say.

What sense do you use? Cut out and paste. Say.

Say. Color the items that begin with /l/ as in *lion*.

Practice

Trace and color. Say /l/ as in *lollipop*.

Our Values

Who is listening to the teacher? Color.

Application/Value: Listen to Your Teacher

Our Senses

Color items you can hear. Circle items you can taste. Say.

Color and say.

Trace. Draw lines and match.

Presentation

Describe the clowns' feelings. Draw a clown.

Practice

Count and say. Cut out and paste.

1

2

3

4

Say. Circle items that begin with /m/ as in *merry-go-round*.

Practice

Say. Match items that begin with /l/ to the *lion*.
Match items that begin with /m/ to the *mother*.

Our Values

Who is kind? Circle.

Application/Value: Be Kind

At the Fair

Match the rides and say.

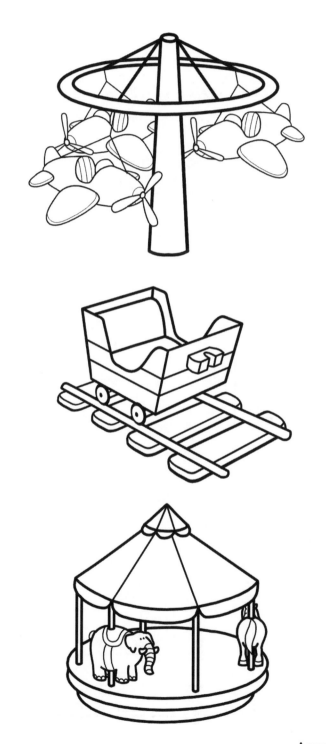

Draw a cousin and a friend.

Warm Up

Point and say: *grandparents, uncle, aunt, cousin.* **Color.**

Who is *tall*? Circle. Draw someone *tall* and someone *short*.

Practice

Trace. Draw the shapes inside the circles.

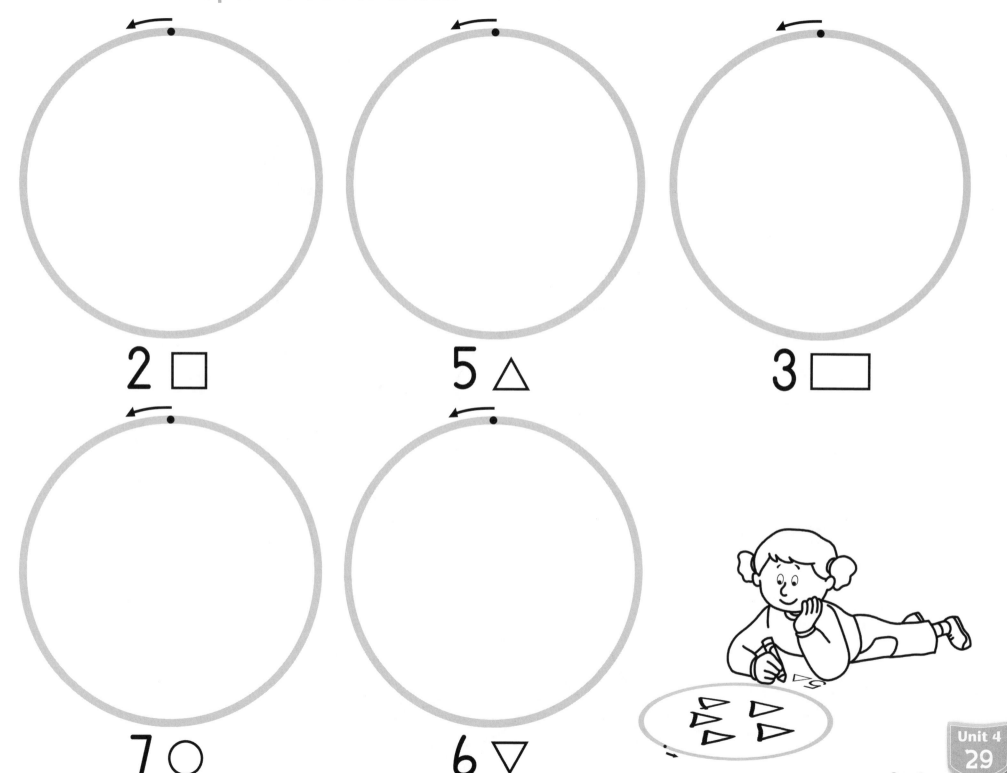

2 □

5 △

3 ▭

7 ○

6 ▽

Trace. Connect the dots in number order and color.

1 2 3 4 5 6 7

Practice

Say. Color items that begin with /f/.

Our Values

She is not telling the truth. Circle a face.

Application/Value: Tell the Truth

People We Know

Draw and color your *aunt* and *uncle*.

Draw a monkey. Color.

Warm Up

Point and say. Draw an animal face in the circle.

Tell where the ball is: *in front of, behind, in, on.*
Draw a seal and a ball in the water.

Practice

Point and count. Trace and write the missing numbers.

Practice

Trace the path. Circle items that begin with /s/ and say.

Practice

Connect the dots in number order. Name the animal. Color.

Our Values

Trace and color the fence.

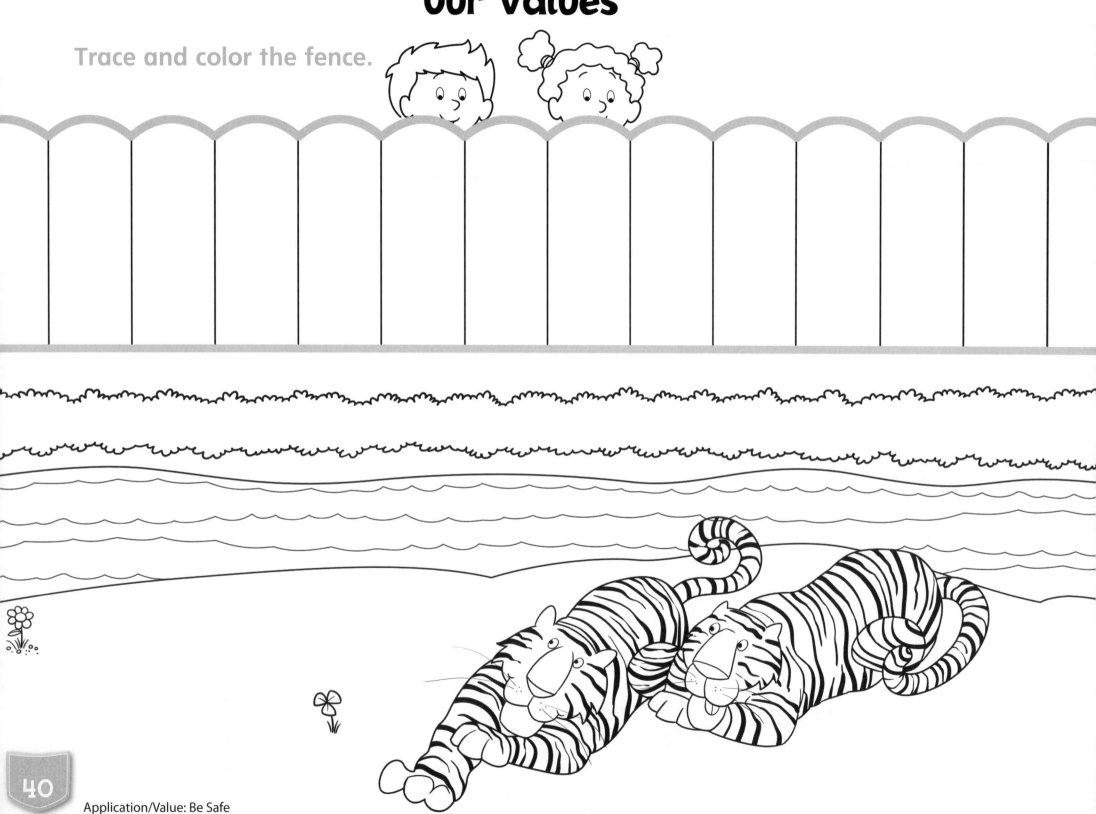

Application/Value: Be Safe

Zoo Animals

Trace. Count and say.

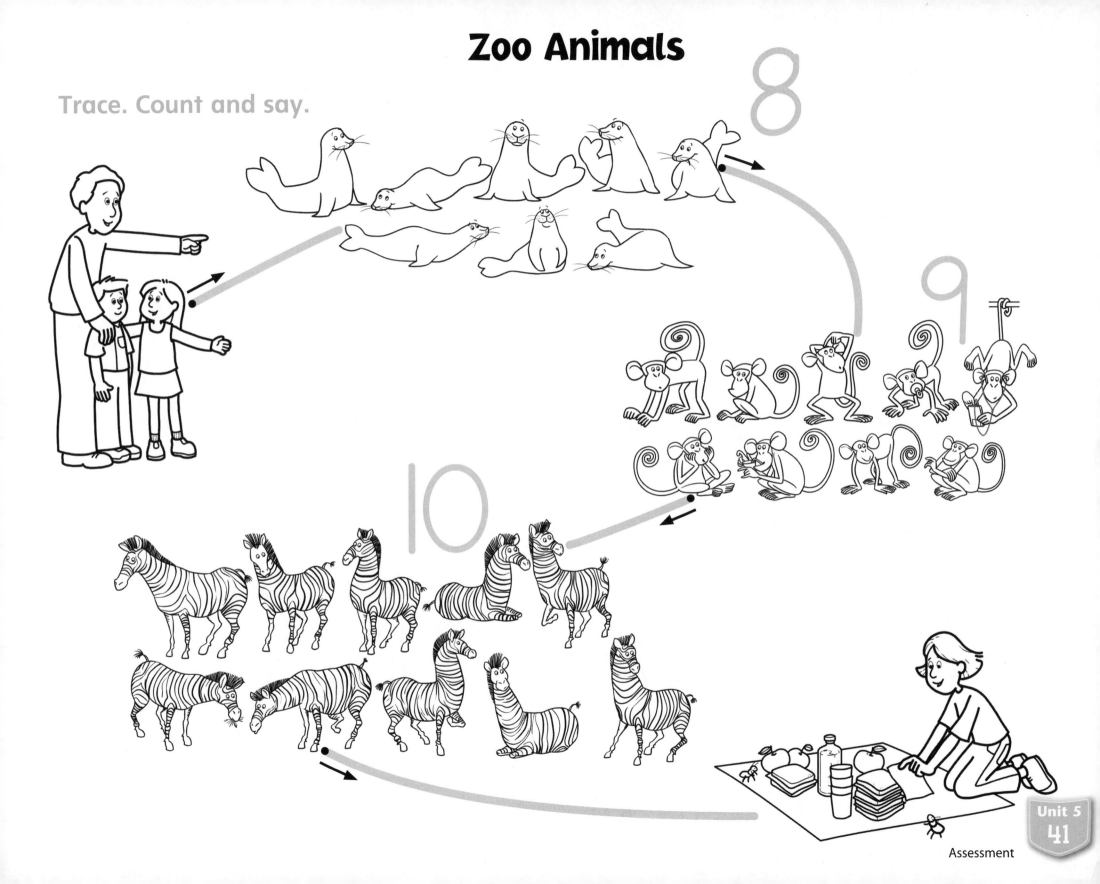

Color the crayons. Then color the clothes.

Warm Up

1  orange 2 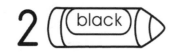 black 3  pink 4  yellow 5  blue

Say. Cut out and paste to match.

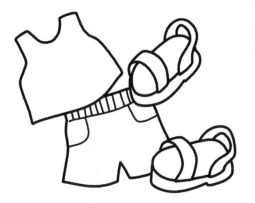

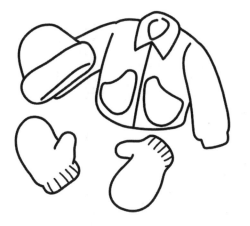

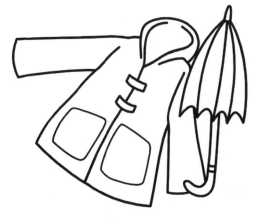

Same or different? Trace the example.
Circle pairs of same shapes. Cross out other pairs.

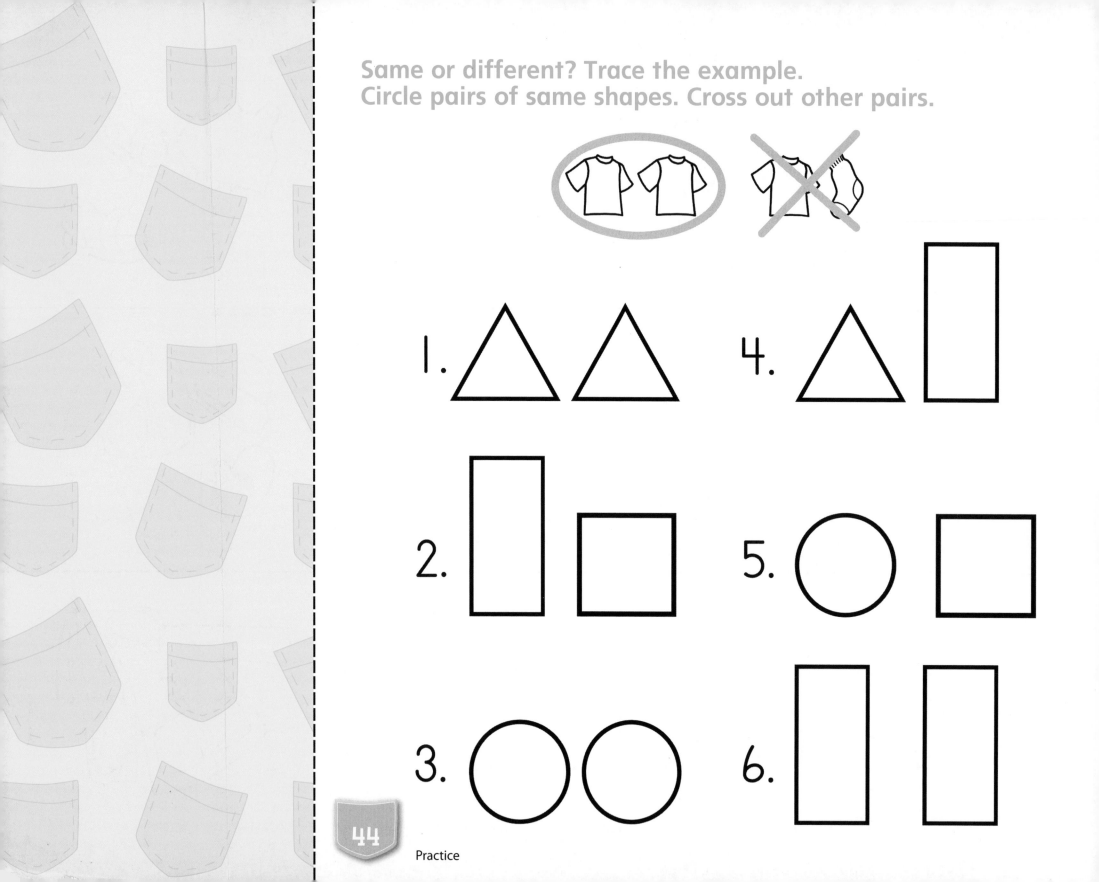

1.

2.

3.

4.

5.

6.

Practice

Count and match. Trace the numbers.

11

12

13

Trace and say. Circle items that begin with /f/.

Practice

Trace and say. Tear paper and paste.

a fish

Our Values

Draw lines to the clean clothes. Say.

Application/Value: Take Care of Your Things

Clothes for All Weather

Draw the weather and say.

What do they want to eat? Draw the foods.

Name the foods. Cut out and paste.

Presentation

Same or different? Trace the example. Circle pairs of same letters. Cross out other pairs.

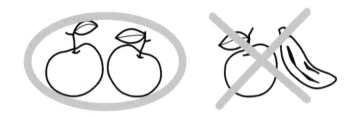

1. A A

2. S E

3. T T

4. C Z

5. B B

6. L K

7. Y H

8. P G

Practice

Count and circle the number. Color.

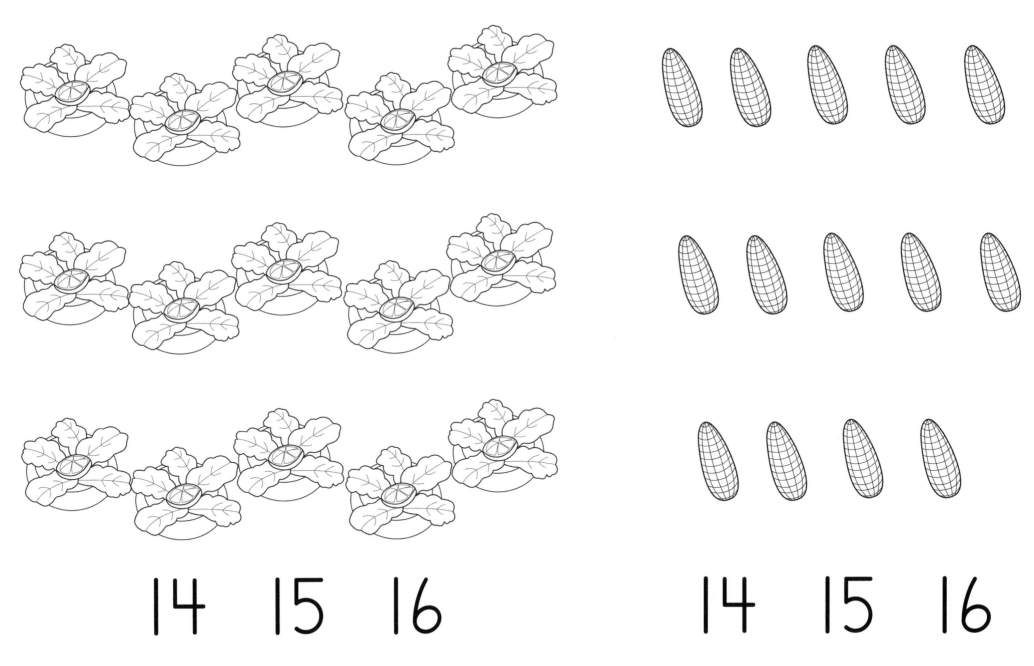

14   15   16

14   15   16

Trace and say. Circle items that begin with /s/.

Practice

What is it? Connect the dots in number order and color. Trace and say.

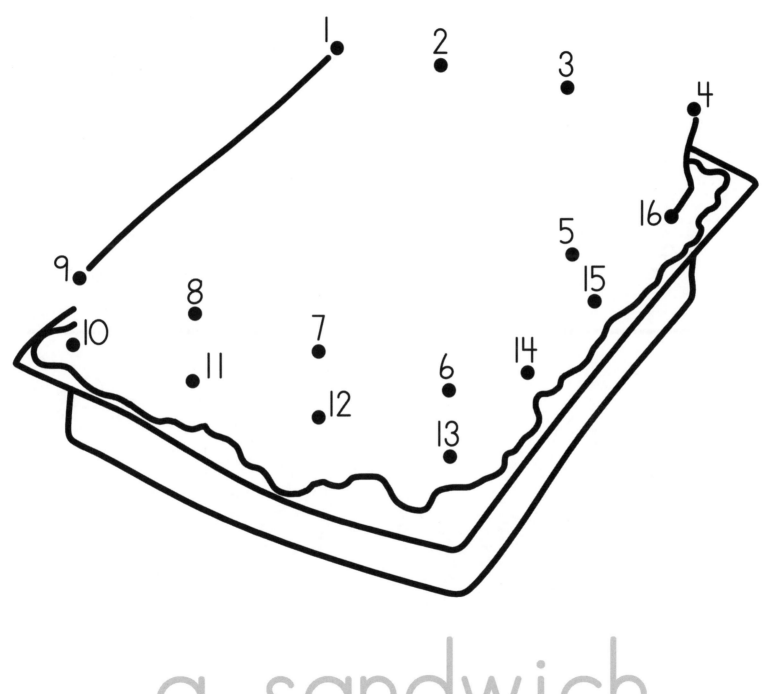

a sandwich

Our Values

Who are polite? Circle.

Application/Value: Be Polite

Foods We Like

Draw foods and drinks for the picnic. Say.

Name each place. Trace. Draw a line from each item to a place.

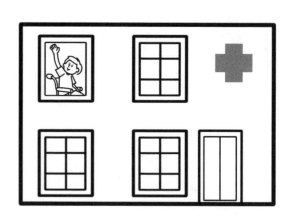

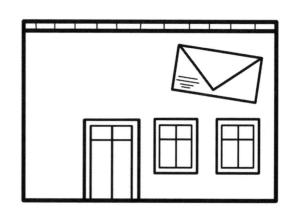

What do you see when you go to each place? Say. Then draw.

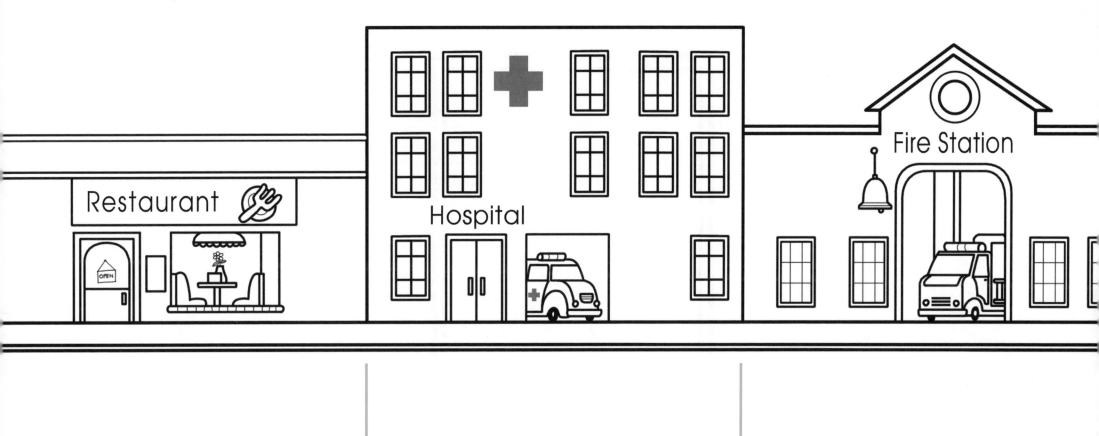

Trace the circles. Color the stoplight red, yellow, and green.

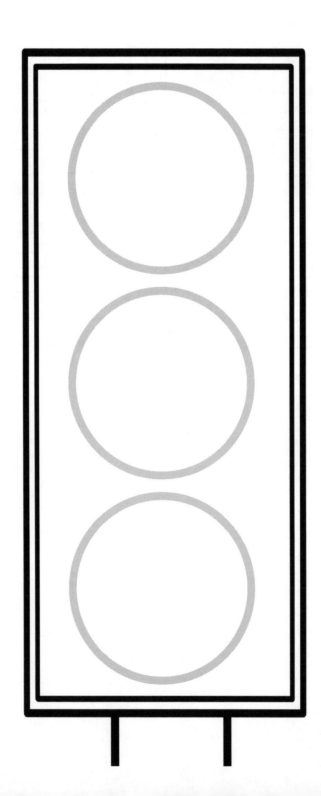

Practice

What is it? Connect the dots in number order. Trace and say.

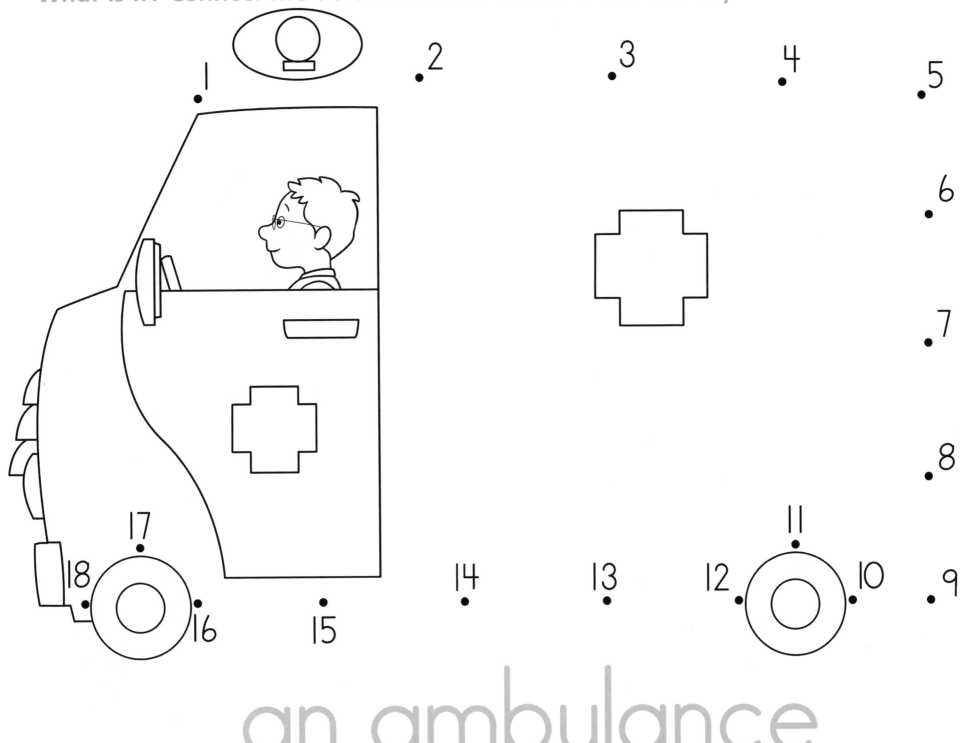

an ambulance

Trace and say. Circle items that begin with /m/.

Practice

Trace the path. Say the letter sound. Circle the item that begins with the same sound.

Our Values

Who is keeping places clean? Circle.

Application/Value: Keep Places Clean

Our Neighborhood

Name the places. Draw someone working at each place.

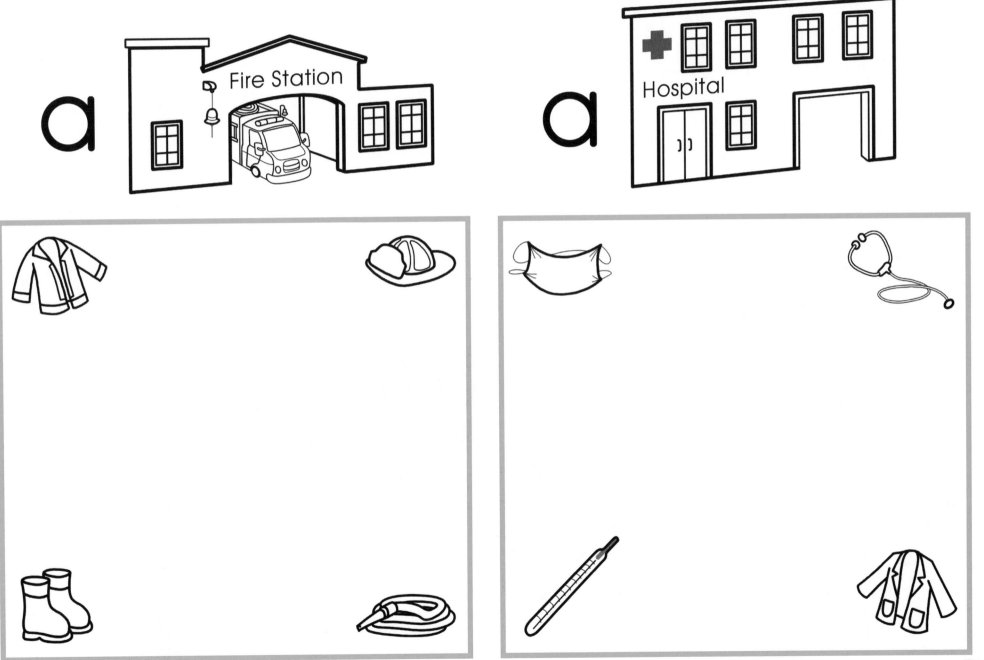

a **Fire Station**

a **Hospital**

Talk about each picture. Draw the sky above each child.

Warm Up

Point and say. Cut out and paste.

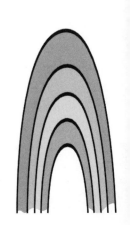

Presentation

What is it? Connect the dots in number order. Trace and say.

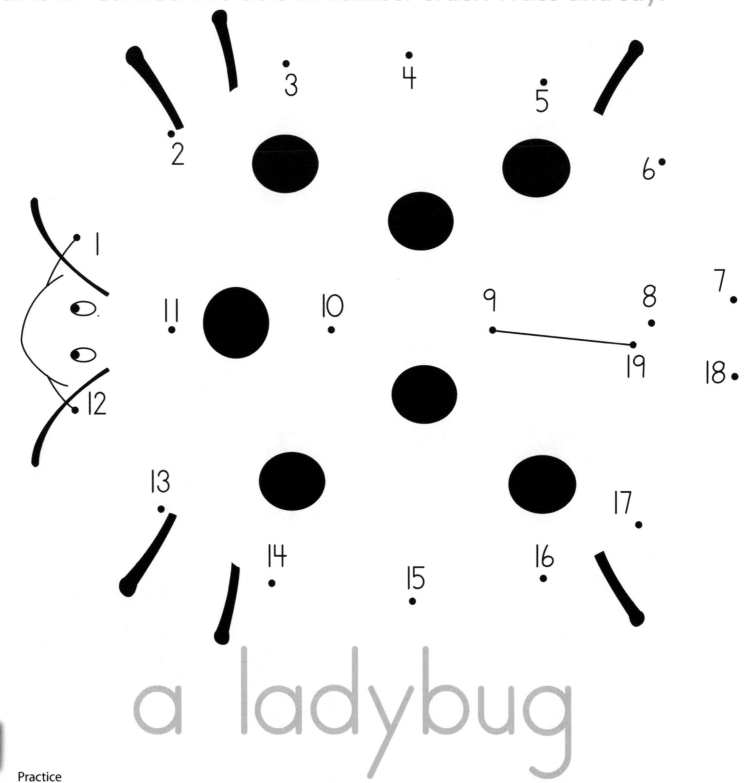

a ladybug

Practice

Follow the path. Trace and say the numbers. Name the items.

Say. Match items that begin with the same sound.

Practice

Match and trace. Then circle the item that begins with the same sound.

Our Values

Trace. Draw more lines to put trash in the trash can.

Application/Value: Respect Nature

The Sky

Trace and color. Draw a crayon and color it.

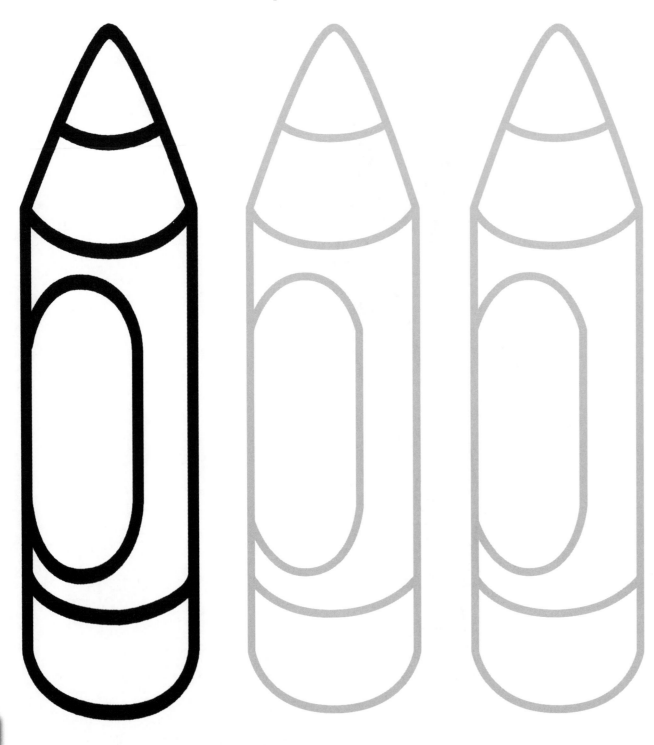

Extra Practice

Cut out and say. Paste pictures that begin with /l/ under the happy lion. Paste others under the sad lion.

77

Trace the parts of the body each boy is using. Say.

Extra Practice

Draw things that begin with /f/. Say.

Find and color the things that begin with /m/. Say.

Extra Practice

✂ **Color the clown. Cut out and fold.
Make the clown *tall* and *short*.**

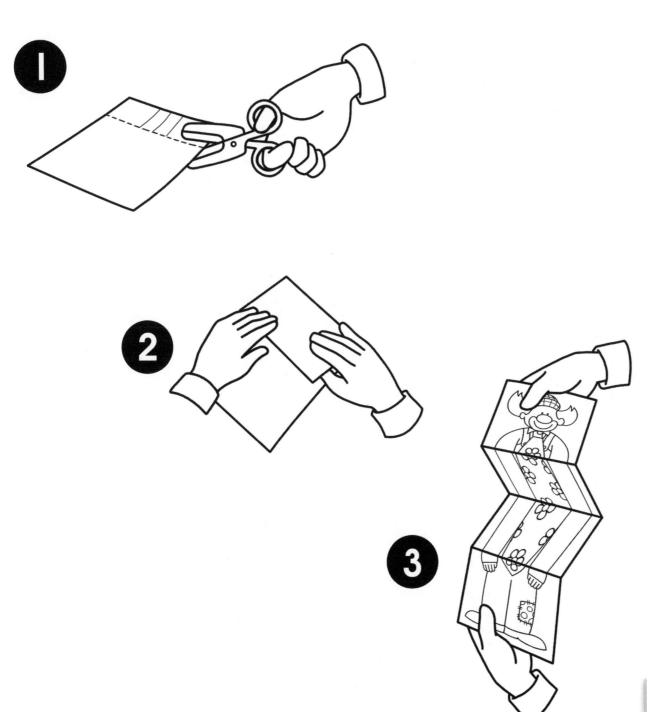

1

2

3

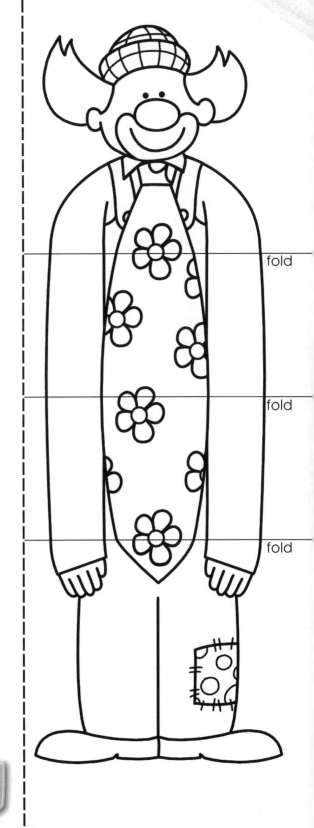

fold

fold

fold

81

Color and cut out. Use the cards for the activity on page 83.

Extra Practice

Use the cards on page 82. Trace the path and say. Match /l/ and /f/ sounds by placing cards on the lions and fish.

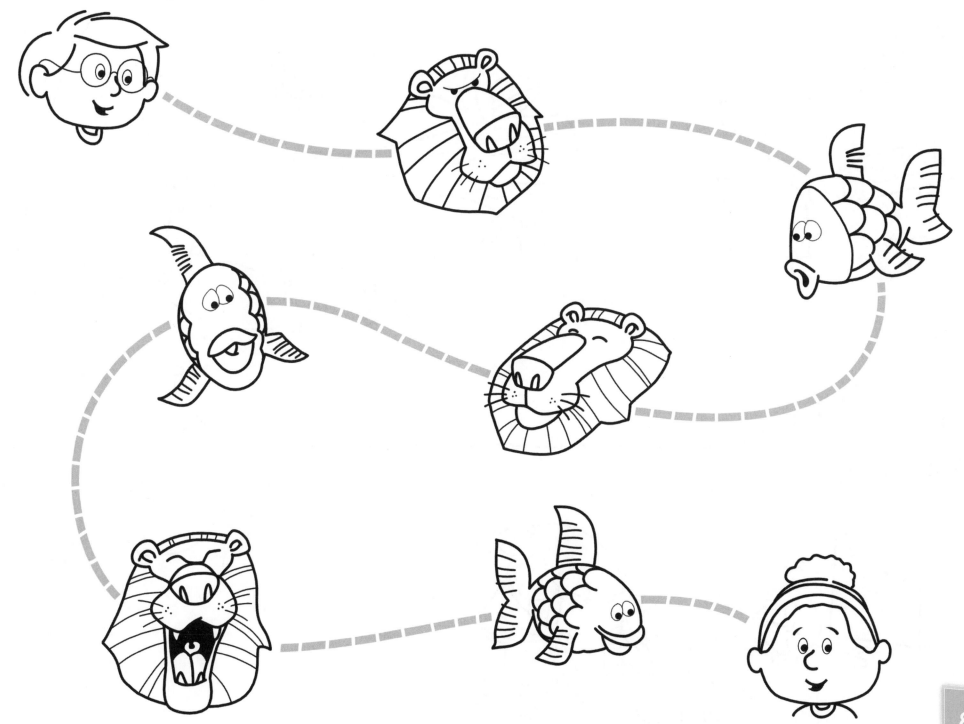

Color the things that begin with /m/ blue.
Color the things that begin with /s/ yellow. Say.

Extra Practice

Trace and cut out the letters. Paste *s* next to the big *S*. Then paste *s* next to the items that begin with /s/.

S

S

S

S

Tell which foods you like and don't like.
Circle the happy face or sad face.

Extra Practice

Trace and cut out the letters. Paste letters that match **M** and **m**. Then paste *m* next to pictures that begin with /m/.

M   m

M

m

m

m

Trace. Draw yourself and friends on the bus. Color.

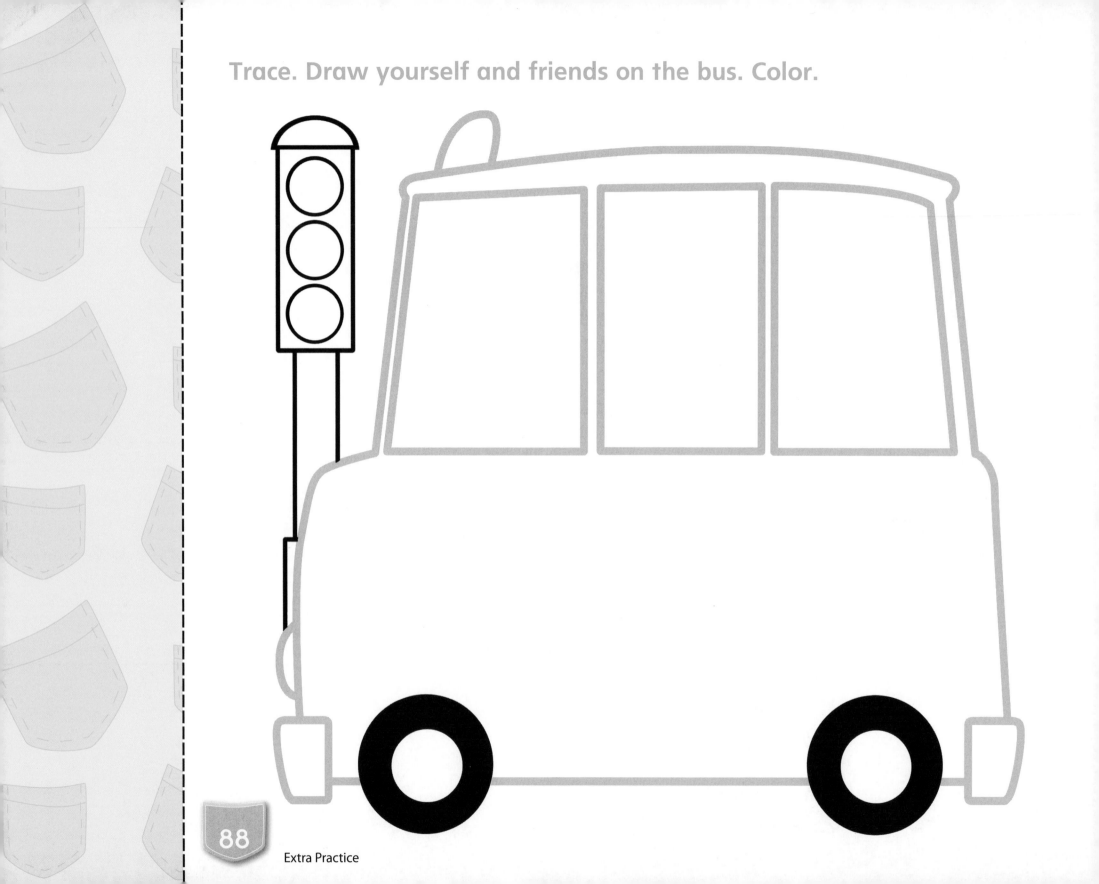

Extra Practice

 Trace. Cut out and match.

F

L

M

S

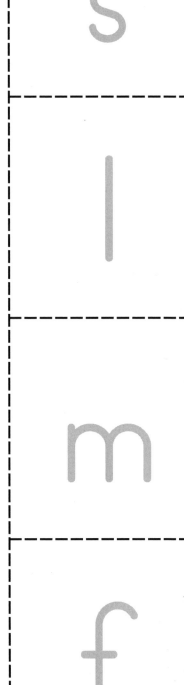

s

l

m

f

Trace. Say and write the letter.

s m l f

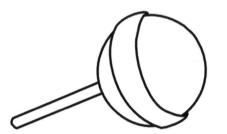

_____

_____

Extra Practice

L l M m

F f S s

Extra Practice

Color and cut out the puppet. Tape or paste the puppet to a stick. Use the puppet for role-plays and conversations.

93

Smiley Tiger Puppet

Smiley Tiger Puppet